Herda, D.J.

AUTHOR

ENVIRONMENTAL American

TITLE

Environmental
AMERICA

Environmental
AMERICA

The Northwestern States

by
D.J. Herda

The Millbrook Press
Brookfield, CT
The American Scene

Cover photographs courtesy of D. J. Herda

Inside photographs courtesy of
U.S. Department of Agriculture Forest Service: 10, 25, 43; U.S. Environmental
Protection Agency: 14, 30, 48, 54; Tom Stack & Associates: 39; U.S. Department of
Energy: 46; D. J. Herda: 6, 13, 18, 26, 34

Designed by Moonlit Ink, Madison, WI 53705
Illustrations by Renee Graef

Cataloging-in-Publication Data
Herda, D. J.
Environmental America: The Northwestern States.
Brookfield, CT, The Millbrook Press. 1991.
64 p.; col. ill.; (The American Scene)
Includes bibliographical references and index.
Summary: The impact of humankind and society on the environment, with special
emphasis on the Northwestern region
ISBN 1-878841-10-6   639.9 HER

1. Northwest states—environmental impacts—juvenile literature. 2. Conservation of
natural resources. 3. Pollution. [1. Environmental America: The Northwestern States]
I Title. II. Series.

CONTENTS

Introduction
7

The Web of LIfe
11

The Land We Walk
19

The Air We Breathe
31

The Water We Drink
35

A Time For Action
43

What We Can Do
51

For More Information
55

Notes
58

Glossary
59

Bibliography
62

Index
63

INTRODUCTION

It's mid-June. Throughout the winding mountains of the American Northwest—Wyoming, Idaho, Montana, Oregon, Washington, and Alaska—wildflowers bloom, animals stir, and geologic formations rise from the land like nowhere else on Earth. Small, babbling creeks and wildly raging rivers crisscross the countryside. Daytime temperatures hover around 80° F, then drop at night to near freezing.

As the sun comes up in the morning, jagged mountains pierce the early blue-gray sky—the Rockies, Bitterroots, Cascades, and other breathtaking ranges with their snow-capped peaks and towering stands of pines.

It's all part of life in the Northwest. But the mountains, while making up a large part of the region's terrain, aren't the area's only natural environment. The region also boasts great stretches of open rangeland, upland foothills laced with tall evergreen trees, and some ranges so high in elevation that no trees at all can grow on them—the tundra. Each distinct environment, or biome, has provided a unique home for a broad variety of plants and animals practically from the beginning of life on Earth.

THE BIRTH OF THE PLANETS

Not all scientists agree on how the Earth was formed. Some speculate that a huge explosion in the cosmos scattered debris in all directions, nine mammoth chunks of which ended up orbiting our sun as planets. Others theorize that the solar system was created when a cloud of gas condensed to form the sun and a group of small planetoids. A series of collisions between these planetoids eventually created larger bodies, finally resulting in the formation of the nine planets, their moons, and numerous asteroids, comets, and meteoroids.[1]

Although the scientific community disagrees on how the Earth was formed, nearly everyone believes that the early

(opposite page)
The majestic Rocky Mountain range dominates the skyline of both Montana and Wyoming.

planet was most likely a molten, lifeless ball of scorching rock. It had no oxygen to sustain life—in fact, no atmosphere at all. There was little or no water vapor, nitrogen, carbon dioxide, methane, hydrogen, or other common Earth gases.

As time passed and the surface of the Earth cooled, those few gases that did exist combined with sunlight, water, and wind to create an environment suitable for simple aquatic plants. These plants used carbon from existing carbon dioxide gas and the energy of the sun to create basic sugars, or carbohydrates, which they turned into food.

As these simple plants flourished, they gave off oxygen. The oxygen, held near the Earth's surface by the planet's gravitational pull, eventually evolved into the atmosphere so necessary to sustain higher forms of life.

HOMO ERECTUS ARRIVES

By the time Homo erectus—our earliest immediate ancestors—evolved on Earth, the dinosaurs and most other large reptiles had long since vanished. They'd been destroyed by massive changes in geography, climate, and sea levels.

Eventually, Homo erectus evolved into Homo sapiens, the species to which all human beings belong. That was approximately 90,000 years ago—a mere tick on the biological clock that stretches back nearly 4.6 billion years![2]

Today, Earth's biosphere—that part of the planet capable of supporting life—is constantly changing. Nearly 1.4 million living species have been identified and named by scientists. Of these, about 750,000 are insects, 265,000 are plants, 41,000 are vertebrates, and the rest are invertebrates such as fungi, algae, and various other microorganisms.[3] But the true number of species on Earth is still unknown. Scientists speculate that there may be as many as 5 to 30 million species or more. In fact, recent studies in tropical forests suggest that there may be as many as 30 million insect species alone. Yet many of these species are disappearing.

Extinctions have happened throughout history, of course. If it weren't for extinctions, giant dinosaurs, saber-toothed tigers, and dodo birds might still walk the Earth. One of the major differences between extinctions thousands of years ago and

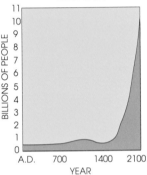

World Population Growth

BILLIONS OF PEOPLE

11
10
9
8
7
6
5
4
3
2
1
0

A.D.   700   1400   2100
YEAR

World population growth and global development are two of the main problems facing the environment.

Sources: Population data from Population Reference Bureau, various publications; historical data from Richard D. Lamm, *Hard Choices* (Denver, CO: May 1985), p. 34

those taking place today, however, is called humanity—the most powerful and destructive force in the history of the Earth. Early extinctions were the result of natural events and evolution; most of today's are human-caused.

Each time a modern plant or animal species vanishes from the planet, the world grows smaller, and its remaining species become more vulnerable. How long can these extinctions continue before humankind destroys the very planet on which we depend for life? A thousand years? A hundred? Fifty?

The answer is unclear. In the meantime, the destruction continues.

The viceroy butterfly is one small example of the fragile community of insects native to the Northwest.

THE WEB OF LIFE

Throughout the Northwest, life struggles to survive. Rocky Mountain oaks grow spindly and stunted in shallow topsoil barely able to adhere to the mountainsides. Ocean shrimp hatch in coastal eddies and provide food for great schools of saltwater fish. Porcupines cling to the very tops of 100-foot lodgepole pines. Algae grow in the scalding hot waters of natural springs.

Although biological species have come into and gone out of existence for hundreds of millions of years, their rate of decline has accelerated greatly since the Industrial Revolution. Plants and animals in the American Northwest have been seriously affected.

OUR RESTLESS EARTH

But the story of the American Northwest, like that of the Earth itself, is much more complex than a tale of vanishing animals. It's the story of tall trees and raging rivers, of massive mountains and sprawling oceans. It's the story of raging forest fires and vast fields of wildflowers. It's the story of the land.

Earth is made up of a core of radioactive metal beneath a layer of molten magma, or hot, liquefied rock. This is covered by a thin, solid crust made of soil.[1]

As the underground magma is excited by "hot spots" in the Earth's core, it moves in currents, much like a stream. Wherever the currents are strongest, the Earth's crust cracks into a jigsaw puzzle of distinct sections, called plates. Over millions of years, these plates have pushed and pulled against one another as they travel across the magma.

(opposite page)
The number of spotted owls in the Northwest once totaled more than 100,000. Today, they're near extinction.

Forests, mountains, grasslands, and oceans lie above this uneasy foundation. Entire continents drift on this mantle of moving magma like icebergs on the surface of the sea. As underground currents drive the plates together or pull them apart, continents bulge, split, collide, and slip along the cracks in the Earth's surface at a rate of an inch or so a year.

As the plates crunch against one another, the Earth's surface buckles and heaves, and small hills are born. Eventually, these swell into mountains.

THE RUSH WEST

The greatest of America's mountain ranges, the Rockies, stopped westward-bound explorers and settlers for years. But they never halted humankind's imagination. What lay beyond this magnificent mountain range? Fabled beasts, lost Indian tribes, the remnants of long-vanished civilizations?

A massive gold strike in the Sierra Nevada foothills finally led settlers by the tens of thousands to California and from there north along the Pacific coast.

Adventurers coming down from the high mountain plateaus settled on the grassy plains and in the foothills of Washington and Oregon, where they began homesteading the land. For them, millions of acres of wilderness held the promise of immense wealth. Soon, homesteaders were locked in a race to see who could import the most livestock and raise the greatest number of cattle and sheep, which they did in ever increasing numbers. Eventually, the number of livestock proved too great for even the richest northwestern lands to support.

The overgrazed grasses soon grew thin and weak. Normal periods of drought turned once-green meadows into barren brown fields of dirt and dust. Sudden rains turned the soil to mud and sent much of it rushing to the sea.

LAND OF PLENTY?

Tens of thousands of homesteaders, each one seeking a share of free land and a brighter future, fought their way through high mountain passes to the promised land of green and plenty.

They brought with them more sheep and cattle and bred increasingly larger herds that placed even more of a strain on newly cleared pasturelands.

Then, during the early 1930s, an era of economic depression struck the country. Farms failed and small businesses collapsed. Many settlers followed old pioneer trails west to the coast, hoping for better fortunes. Some became migrant farm workers, others fishermen, prospectors, oilmen, and ranchers. Still others turned to logging.

Large farms and increasing numbers of livestock place a growing strain on the Northwest's environment.

LOGGING IN THE NORTHWEST

"Everywhere a man could see were trees as high as heaven," one logger boasted in a letter home after making his way to the city of Portland, Oregon, from Minneapolis, Minnesota. And he was right. The greatest concentration of trees in America crowded the hills and valleys of the Northwest.

In addition to the prospect of providing homes for thousands of people, the forests provided protection for watersheds, regulated water flow, influenced weather patterns, and helped prevent soil erosion and the pollution of rivers with sedimentary runoff. They also provided a rich source of food, fibers, and wood for building; fuel for cooking, lighting, and heating; and animal fodder for livestock.

During the years following the Civil War, the timber industry in the eastern and central United States had been weakened by overcutting and poor management. Instead of selectively removing old, crowded, or diseased trees to enable the remaining forest to continue producing wood for future generations, loggers clear-cut hundreds of thousands of acres, leveling every tree in their wake. It was the cheapest, easiest, and most environmentally destructive way to harvest wood.

And when the great forests of the eastern and central states were gone, the loggers turned their gaze toward the Northwest.

THE DESTRUCTION OF THE FORESTS

As with other industries, logging in the Northwest was profit-driven. "The only good tree," one logging camp foreman boasted, "is a dead tree."

And trees in the Northwest died by the millions as loggers systematically cut the forests from one end of the region to the other with little thought toward the consequences. Beginning in those areas where the timber was thickest and the means to get at it easiest, they quickly clear-cut huge stands of native pine and other trees and sent the logs downstream to a sawmill. There they were carved into rough lumber and loaded onto horse-drawn wagons, trucks, or railway cars for delivery to market.

(opposite page)
Although an important northwestern industry, logging today threatens the region's forest environment.

World Land Area Suitable for Agriculture

No Limitations	11%
Too Wet	10%
Too Shallow	22%
Chemical Problems	23%
Too Dry	28%
Unaccounted	6%

Satellite topographical studies show that, of all the world's land, very little is actually suitable for agricultural use.

Source: Essam, El-Hinnawi and Mansur, Hashmi, *The State of the Environment* (London: Butterworths, 1987), p. 36

As these turn-of-the-century "brushrats" slowly worked their way east from the coast and west from the central United States, all but the least accessible forests of the mountainous regions of the Northwest fell to the bucksaw, ax, and chainsaw. In many cases, this broad-scale butchery of one of our nation's richest resources was supported and sometimes even subsidized by local governments. It was also backed by ranchers who wanted the forests cleared so that they could graze more sheep and cattle on the newly opened lands.

As natural forest habitat disappeared and ranchers took over the lands, timber wolves and grizzly bears, which once roamed the entire Northwest, were shot on sight in a misguided effort to prevent rare attacks on young or diseased livestock. The population of northwestern deer, moose, and elk likewise declined as a result of hunting for both food and sport and from the destruction of their natural habitat.

The American bison, which once numbered 60 million head, was slaughtered for both food and hides until, by 1900, it tottered on the very brink of extinction. Numerous species of birds, including many hawks, eagles, and owls, also grew scarce.

Today, only 725,000 of 3.2 million acres of original spotted owl habitat in western Washington and Oregon remain. Most of that is in designated wilderness areas. Only 28 known breeding pairs of owls currently exist—each pair of which requires up to 4,500 acres for survival. As unprotected forestlands continue to be logged, biologists fear that soon the remaining owls will be too isolated and inbred to ensure the survival of the species.

As nearly all species of native wildlife declined in the Northwest during the first four decades of the twentieth century, a few non-native species prospered. These included animals such as sheep, goats, hogs, cattle and human beings.

FAILING PASTURELANDS

Ironically, even domestic livestock began to decrease in number as the relentless clearing of northwestern lands took its toll. Soil erosion, compaction by both cattle and farm vehicles, and the periodic burning of native grasses to control the

spread of weeds resulted in acre after acre of lifeless, worthless scrublands where once some of the richest timberlands in the world had stood. Ranchers with thousands of head of livestock to graze cut a path deeper and deeper into former forestlands in a constant search for greener pastures.

Once millions of bison roamed the plains. Today, they're struggling to escape extinction.

In less than half a century, humankind in its ignorance had upset the balance of nature and destroyed rich stands of native trees. Where once endless forests of native pines swayed gently in the wind, sagebrush, Canadian thistle, and other useless shrubs and weeds soon dotted the countryside.

Today, the devastation continues. In many areas, it's escalating. If this trend continues, more than one fifth of the world's species may not exist by the turn of the century.

How much interference from humankind can nature tolerate? Where will the destruction to our environment end? Unless something is done soon to stop it, we may find ourselves living in a world much less diverse than it is today. And that could spell disaster for our future.

THE LAND WE WALK

Throughout the American Northwest, a wide range of wildlife still exists, from grizzlies and wolves to bighorn sheep, coyotes, cougars, bison, kit foxes, elf owls, mountain jays, and mourning doves.

All of these animals are interdependent on each other and their environment for life. All of them are part of nature's food chain—a complex interrelationship that begins at the very bottom of the life scale.

THE FOOD CHAIN

Soil in the Northwest varies greatly in content, from the dry, sandy soils of the lowland deserts to the rich, humus-filled soils of the highland Pacific forestlands. From healthy soils grow healthy plants. These plants serve as a rich source of vitamins and minerals for a wide variety of insects and animals, from microscopic mites to deer, antelope, and bison.

A typical food chain in the Northwest may begin with a single blade of grass. A cricket feeds on the grass; a frog feeds on the cricket; a salmon feeds on the frog; an eagle feeds on the salmon; a mountain lion feeds on the eagle. If any one element in the food chain is disrupted, the entire chain could be upset, possibly with permanent damage.

Plants also play an important role in the lives of human beings. Without green plants, we'd have no beef, butter, cheese, milk, or yogurt, all of which can be traced down the food chain back to plants. We'd have no grain-eating chickens to supply us with eggs. Even fish that live off smaller fish that in turn live off plants called algae would soon disappear.

(opposite page)
Large stands of evergreen forests like this one near Portland, Oregon, are becoming scarce.

UPSETTING THE LAND

By the turn of the century, most of the great forests that once blanketed the eastern and midwestern American states had been systematically destroyed. A few wealthy timber barons had harvested all the marketable trees and burned what remained, then turned the land over to livestock. Soon, nearly all the great forests of the region had disappeared. With them went acorn-eating passenger pigeons and cypress-seed-eating Carolina parakeets. Once their habitat had been destroyed, they were doomed to extinction.

Water supplies dwindled, too, as clear-cut lands with little or no remaining vegetation to absorb and hold rain produced unpredictable cycles of floods and drought.

In response to such devastation, Congress decided to act. Under the Forest Reserve and Organic Administration Acts of 1891 and 1897, the president was authorized to set aside forest reserves to secure "favorable conditions of water flows, and furnish a continuous supply of timber." During the administration of Theodore Roosevelt, the federal government designated over 100 million acres of national forest and created a Forest Service to manage them.

Slowly, America's eastern and central forestlands began to reappear. Animals such as the white-tailed deer that had been chased from most of the East returned under federal protection. Wood ducks once again were nesting in the trees—but in wooden duck boxes provided by wildlife managers to replace the old-growth trees (trees that have lived since the days of America's colonization) that the ducks had once used as homes.

LOGGERS DISCOVER THE NORTHWEST

Logging companies that sent out scouts to examine the possibility of logging the Northwest were delighted with the reports. Throughout Oregon, Washington, and Idaho, mile after mile of virgin pine forests stood waiting for the ax and saw. In Montana and Wyoming, more sprawling stands of mature timber beckoned. And in Alaska, the trees were as thick as oats in a midwestern farmer's field.

It didn't take the logging industry long to begin cutting roads into the wilderness and churning out fresh timber. At first, the going was slow. But as equipment and men poured into the Northwest, old-growth forests that had stood for thousands of years fell almost overnight.

By 1960, total lumber production in the United States had topped 33 billion board feet (a commonly used measurement for lumber). By 1987 that figure had skyrocketed more than 33 percent to nearly 45 billion board feet.

Alarmed by the swiftness with which logging had taken hold in the Northwest, the U.S. Forest Service began setting aside large wilderness and primitive areas where logging was to be banned indefinitely. Then came the baby boom following World War II. Human population, already increasing rapidly because of improvements in health care and nutrition, took a sudden leap, doubling in less than 50 years. Where would the necessary houses come from? The furniture? The food?

In response to increasing demands, the Forest Service opened millions of acres of Northwest old-growth timberlands to intensive logging. Loggers clear-cut entire mountainsides, removing every living tree. They bulldozed the ground clean in preparation for grazing cattle or replanting the land with fast-growing commercial species such as Douglas fir. Except for the massive scale of the operation, it looked from the air like a Kansas wheat farmer harvesting his fields.

As conservationists around the world grew alarmed, the service defended its policies. But the critics believed that removing old-growth forests and replacing them with huge crops of same-age trees was unwise. Old-growth forests produce far more fruit and nuts for wildlife than do young trees. They also provide more nesting sites and better shelter.

The critics turned out to be right. Throughout the Northwest, numerous animal species that once relied on old-growth forests have been pushed to the brink of extinction. The spotted owl, which depends on old-growth coniferous trees for habitat, now has trouble finding rodents such as flying squirrels and tree voles that constitute a major portion of its diet. In addition, clear-cutting destroys the natural forest canopy that provides the spotted owl with protection from larger birds of prey, such as the great horned owl. It seems unlikely that the spotted owl will survive current logging practices.

Despite growing objections to the cutting of old-growth timber, the Forest Service has continued selling logging rights to practically anyone interested in buying them—often for far less money than it spends putting in logging roads and preparing the forests for harvest. In 1987, nearly 13 billion board feet of timber were cut on national forestlands—much of it old-growth timber—an all-time record. More than 5.5 billion board feet were taken from the Northwest alone—another all-time record and a rate that conservationists insist is disastrous.

"We Americans preach a double standard," according to National Wildlife Federation president Jay D. Hair. "We've been denouncing nations like Brazil for the destruction of its rain forests, and yet we continue to do the same to our last stands of ancient forests."

A NEW FOREST PLAN

Meanwhile, in order to meet anticipated growing demands for the future, the Forest Service is struggling to fulfill its logging plan for the next half century. Included in its controversial plan is the intention to remove as much historic timber as possible from 19 national forests in the Pacific Northwest. To make matters worse, the plan proposes cutting more timber than would be replaced by new growth in five of America's 19 national forests.

In response, the National Wildlife Federation has issued a document outlining its opposition to the service's plan. The document pointed out that increasing numbers of citizens value their national forests not just for their commercial timber value, but also for the relief they offer from the pressures of city life, as well as for "the homes for wildlife they provide, the clean water they assure us, and the sheer magnificence of their natural beauty."

In an unexpected move apparently meant to satisfy environmentalists, the service agreed to halt logging operations in some old-growth areas of Idaho not already served by logging roads. It also canceled a scheduled timber sale near that state's

(opposite page)
In 1987, the U.S. Forest Service sold off 13 billion board feet of national forestland timber, an all-time record that has environmentalists alarmed.

Lake Pend Oreille, one of the largest and most popular tourist attractions in the Northwest.

But for every step forward taken in the name of the environment, the Forest Service takes two steps back in the name of development.

ALASKA'S WOES

Southeastern Alaska, a scenic region of islands, bays, coves, fjords, and mountains, hosts the greatest concentration of bald eagles in the world. The birds build massive nests in the crowns of 200-foot-high spruce and hemlock trees that have stood since the Middle Ages.

In the forest below, grizzly bears waddle through the woods and along salmon-filled streams. On Alaska's Admiralty Island, the grizzlies are nearly twice as numerous as in all the lower 48 states combined, where millions of dollars a year are spent to save the remaining bears. Besides grizzlies, the forests are filled with black-tailed deer, Vancouver Canada geese, Steller's jays, chestnut-backed chickadees, red-breasted sapsuckers, and blue grouse.

Each year, the federal government gives millions of dollars to the U.S. Forest Service so it can cut timber in Tongass National Forest in southeastern Alaska. This timber is converted to pulp and shipped to the Orient. According to David Cline, the National Audubon Society's vice president for Alaska, "In my sixteen years of work in Alaska, this is the most serious threat to the environment I've seen."

The Forest Service defends its stand, claiming that logging America's public forestlands is well within its rights. Yet few can understand why the service continues to sell huge amounts of irreplaceable old-growth timber at a tremendous financial loss. The practice is destroying America's most pristine wilderness.

The Lisianski River region, containing some of the finest wild salmon streams in the world, produces more than $400,000 worth of commercial salmon a year. It's also extremely valuable as a sport-fishing area. But the Forest Service wants the region's trees, so it has developed plans to log the Lisianski River corridor. The damage to the streams could spell disaster

for the fishing industry there. The price the government will get for the timber makes the project an even worse value.

At current rates, the timber along the river would bring the federal government approximately $40,000. In turn, the Forest Service will need to spend $1.6 million for forest roads to reach the timber and another $1.4 million in miscellaneous expenses, bringing its total investment to $3 million before the first board foot is removed.

The value to the environment of maintaining the Lisianski River in its wild state, on the other hand, is "at least $445,000 a year," according to Bar Koehler, executive director of the Southeastern Alaska Conservation Council.

Says Oregon's Jim Weaver after sitting through extensive hearings on the Alaska forestry situation, "It's unbelievable. These companies don't even make much money on this. We're just desecrating the Tongass, not for economics, not for community stability, not for employment. We're just doing it."

Conservationists fear that overcutting Alaska's forestlands could spell disaster for wildlife species such as the northern bald eagle.

Unless the Forest Service shows an unexpected reversal in its overall philosophy of forest management, the Northwest will soon have fewer and fewer irreplaceable old-growth forests, along with a dwindling number of wildlife species that make their home in these forests.

THE HIGH ENERGY TOLL

Another polluter of northwestern land is the energy industry. Oil, in particular, has taken its toll as numerous wells have leaked toxic oil, chemicals, and wastewater back into the environment.

After gigantic oil discoveries were made in Alaska, plans were undertaken to build a massive pipeline for delivering the oil to tankers. Environmentalists strongly disapproved. After years of legal battles, the oil companies were granted the right to drill, providing they stayed within certain Environmental Protection Agency (EPA) guidelines. These guidelines were designed to protect Alaska's rich environmental heritage. But today, years after the pipelines began delivering oil, the oil companies have failed to live up to their responsibilities.

Late in 1987, California Congressman George Miller, heading the House Interior Committee evaluating the Prudhoe Bay, Alaska, oil-development experience, discovered that the environmental damage at the bay was much worse than anyone had thought.

An Interior Department report, completed in December 1987, offered some startling insights into how the pipeline had affected the Alaskan wilderness. Although the environmental impact study of the project had foreseen the destruction of 6,000 acres of Alaskan wildlife habitat, more than 11,000 acres—nearly twice the original estimate—had been destroyed. Where no freshwater withdrawals were predicted, over 200 million gallons a year had been used. Where oil companies guaranteed to hold erosion and oil spills to a minimum, the damage had actually been frequent and extensive.

To make matters worse, the Interior Department had suppressed the facts as long as possible, according to Miller, to allow Congress time to vote in favor of a bill opening Alaska's Arctic refuge to oil exploration. A vote on the Arctic bill,

(opposite page)
This solitary Wyoming well pumps oil around the clock.

which could jeopardize even more of Alaska's wildlife in the future, has since been postponed pending additional studies.

BLACKFOOT'S LAST STAND

Outside Montana's Glacier National Park, the Blackfoot Indians and various conservation groups are worried about another proposal by the Forest Service. This one would give Chevron and American Petrofina corporations preliminary approval to drill two exploratory oil and gas wells and build 17 miles of roads in the heart of the region. Chevron officials admit that they're unlikely to find oil or gas there; but if they should, they would need up to 22 wells, a large, rambling network of access roads, and a refinery on the border of the park, according to U.S. Forest Service projections.

To stop the development, the Blackfeet recently joined with conservation clubs and have submitted a plan to have the area designated as a federal wilderness reserve. That would halt future oil and gas development. But both groups admit their chances for holding off the oil companies indefinitely are slim.

NUCLEAR WASTE

Another even more serious form of land pollution facing the Northwest is radioactive waste from nuclear power and nuclear weapons plants. Idaho's Snake River region boasts one of the nation's largest concentrations of cowboys, farmers, and nuclear plant workers. The Department of Energy (DOE) recently proposed building a $1 billion Special Isotope Separation (SIS) project there using laser technology to purify plutonium, one of the deadliest radioactive substances known.

The plant, scheduled to be built at the Idaho National Engineering Laboratory near Idaho Falls, would sit just 530 feet above the Snake River Aquifer. From there, according to concerned environmentalists, it would regularly release into the aquifer such chemicals as carbon tetrachloride, a dangerously toxic solvent used in the plutonium purification process. Idaho farmers currently use water from the aquifer to irrigate their potato crops, and more than 40 nearby communities rely on that same water for drinking.

Toxic Substances Discharged by U.S. Industry, 1987

Destination	Millions of Pounds
Air	2700
Lakes, Rivers and Streams	550
Landfills and Earthen Pits	3900
Treatment and Disposal Facilities	3300
Total	10450

Source: Environmental Protection Agency, reported in *The Washington Post*, April 13, 1989, p. A33

Opponents of the project say the nation has a large enough supply of plutonium without the proposed plant. Even former energy secretary John S. Herrington agrees. "We're awash in plutonium," he told a congressional committee in 1988. "We have more than we need."

Officials at DOE, however, insist that the country needs additional options for producing weapons-grade plutonium.

Despite DOE's objections, opponents of the plant have convinced Congress to delay the start of construction to allow time for further evaluation.

"Local politicians' ears are now open," according to Liz Paul, coordinator of the Snake River Alliance, a nuclear and environmental watchdog group. "If we don't get the project killed this year [1989], we'll be back next year, and the next ... until we do."

Meanwhile, President Bush announced early in 1990 that he had decided not to request funds to build the plant. That decision, according to a March 11, 1990, article in the *New York Times Magazine*, effectively kills the project for the near future.

THE AIR
WE BREATHE

Acid rain begins in the Northwest when automobile exhausts and industrial smokestacks pour tons of pollutants into the air each year. The acidic compounds may fall to Earth and kill off rainbow trout in a mountain lake in Montana or Wyoming. In fact, airborne pollutants may travel thousands of miles before raining down to cause damage.

Research done by the EPA and the Environmental Defense Fund indicates that as many as 2,000 lakes in the Rocky Mountains could be ruined by "as little as one tenth as much acid as needed to acidify some less sensitive lakes in the northeastern United States or Scandinavia." Once a mountain lake becomes acidified, it may take hundreds of years for it to recover sufficiently to support life.

Acid rain also affects hundreds of thousands of acres of prime northwestern forestland, where the short-term effects of the problem are just beginning to be understood. Hardy, fast-growing pines have become stunted. Green, healthy-looking needles have turned pale brown and yellow and eventually fallen off. No one yet knows the long-term effects acid rain will have on some of the world's most valuable virgin forests.

While most of the acid rain in the Northwest comes from industrial smokestacks and automobile exhausts from the region's major cities, a surprisingly large percentage of it may come from other, less obvious, sources.

(opposite page)
Acid rain from industrial smokestacks pollutes the air and threatens the Northwest's most sensitive waterways.

ACID RAIN FROM WOOD FIRES

The thin plumes of smoke rising from a few widely scattered wood stoves and fireplaces enrich the scent of the sweet fall air. It's the smell of small-town life before the turn of the century, of fresh apple pie baking in the oven, of falling leaves of auburn, yellow, and brown.

But when those plumes are multiplied by hundreds or even thousands of fires all squeezed into an area the size of Missoula, Montana, the results are anything but idyllic.

In Missoula, the old-fashioned wood-burning stove is in trouble. Sulfides—a major ingredient in acid rain—pour out of the city's flues faster than the environment can absorb them. So, too, do deadly carbon monoxide and microscopic particles of incompletely burned wood known as polycyclic organic matter, classified by the EPA as carcinogenic.

As a result, Missoula, along with other cities and towns throughout the Northwest, is cracking down. When a light mounted atop the city's water tower flashes to warn residents of an air-pollution alert, all wood fires must be snuffed out. Violators are subject to stiff fines.

As an added step to clean up smoke-befouled air, the federal government recently enacted stricter national standards for emissions by new wood-burning stoves and fireplace inserts. The latest models are equipped with catalytic converters to reduce their output of sulfides, carbon monoxide, and harmful particulates.

Although the catalytic converters increase the price of new wood burners, most citizens find that paying the extra price is better than the alternative—adding to the problems of air pollution and acid rain or else banning wood burners altogether.

So far, the pollution alerts and improved wood burner units are working. Missoula and many of its sister cities throughout the Northwest are awakening to cleaner air.

AGRICULTURAL BURNING

Although wood-burning stoves and fireplaces threaten the atmosphere of communities throughout the Northwest, other forms of air pollution may have even farther-reaching effects. Each summer, 800 farmers in Willamette Valley, Oregon, plant nearly 400,000 acres of grass seed. Following harvest, they set fire to the fields in order to sterilize them and eliminate nearly a million tons of straw waste a year.

Last year, Willamette Valley farmers sold more than $170 million worth of rye, fescue, and other grass-seed varieties for use around the world—from English churchyards to the Rose Bowl—making it the state's fourth largest cash crop.

But Oregon state senator Grattan Kerans and others are upset. "The farmers are avoiding the expense of waste disposal, pocketing their savings, and calling it profit. The public pays the cost."

And the cost is more than money. Burning straw produces sulfides that contribute to the production of acid rain, as well as carcinogenic smoke containing microscopic particulates that irritate the lungs. In addition, many of the fields are regularly treated with fungicides, herbicides, or insecticides, and they, too, go up in smoke.

In 1979, a plan to phase out the burning was scrapped by the state legislature as alternatives to the problem were sought. And so the burning continues. Meanwhile, several environmental groups are preparing a lawsuit against the state to force Oregon to meet the standards of the Clean Air Act.

However the matter is ultimately resolved, the debate over grass-seed burning is only the beginning of a battle against other types of agricultural and timber burning. "The air in this state and beyond is continually polluted by all this burning," says one environmentalist, "making life miserable for hundreds of thousands of people. It has to stop."

CHAPTER FOUR

THE WATER WE DRINK

The Northwest is a rich resource of water—pristine mountain lakes, lowland ponds and streams, roaring canyon rivers. Yet every day, northwestern waterways are exposed to countless sources of water pollution. Today, many of these waters are fighting for their very lives.

POLYAROMATIC HYDROCARBONS

In the 1960s, the surgeon general began warning Americans about the dangers of cigarette smoking. One of the dozens of toxic culprits in cigarettes is a class of deadly carcinogens, or cancer-causing chemicals, known as polyaromatic hydrocarbons (PAHs). PAHs are a by-product of burning organic materials such as tobacco, oil, coal, and wood. They're created by various chemical manufacturing processes, coal gasification facilities (for turning coal into gas), and aluminum plants. They come from sewage, oil, and gas leaked from pleasure boats, as well as from automobile exhaust emissions.

When PAHs enter waterways by way of household and industrial sewage and urban runoff, the result is an alarmingly high quantity of PAH pollution in the food chain. And it all starts at the bottom.

"We're spewing hundreds of tons of PAHs into aquatic ecosystems every year," says biochemist Donald Malins of the Pacific Northwest Research Foundation in Seattle. Because the chemicals tend to bind to heavier suspended particles that eventually sink to the bottom, PAH concentrations are heaviest in ocean and lake sediment. This is especially true along the shorelines of urban and industrial areas.

(opposite page)
Scenic northwestern lakes like this could soon be overrun by chemicals and other pollutants.

35

Fish containing high levels of polyaromatic hydrocarbons have been found in many of the nation's lakes and oceans. In the Northwest, PAHs are most heavily concentrated in Puget Sound, where sediment from industrial polluters has created concentrations 150 times higher than average.

In Eagle Harbor, just west of Seattle, scientists discovered that nearly one fourth of the English sole (a type of fish) sampled contained liver tumors. One of the major contributors to the problem was a large chemical creosote plant.

Recent studies suggesting that PAHs can climb the food chain have fueled new concerns about contamination. One study showed high levels of PAHs attached to the DNA molecules in the brains of dead beluga whales that had washed ashore on Canada's heavily polluted St. Lawrence River. The whales' diet consists mainly of bottom-dwelling fish and invertebrates. One whale had the first bladder cancer ever found in a whale. Evidence points to PAHs producing bladder cancer in human beings, as well.

To date, little has been done about PAHs in the Northwest. This is partly because contamination by the toxins has only recently been discovered and partly because scientists are still debating the most effective means of combatting them.

MINING POLLUTANTS

Strip mining for coal takes its toll on the Northwest's waterways, too. The drainage from mining operations in Oregon, Washington, Wyoming, and Montana pollutes thousands of miles of streams and rivers. This drainage, which is highly acidic, harms or kills living organisms and corrodes metal structures. Iron compounds in the drainage coat the bottoms of streams, lakes, and rivers, making them uninhabitable.

Sulfides in the drainage combine with oxygen to form sulfates and sulfuric acid. Water running through the mines carries the acidic compounds into both underground and surface water systems, where they poison aquatic organisms and damage the ecosystem.

The U.S. Department of the Interior estimates it would cost between $7 billion and $12 billion to clean up all U.S. waterways polluted by strip-mining. Yet despite environmental concerns, strip-mining in the Northwest is on the increase as the country's reliance on coal as a cheap, plentiful source of energy grows. Even though both federal and state regulations govern various aspects of strip mining, not enough is being done to protect northwestern waterways.

AGRICULTURAL POLLUTANTS

During the 1940s, '50s, and '60s, U.S. farmers turned increasingly to chemical pesticides and fertilizers to improve the condition of their crops. Even though such toxic pesticides as DDD and DDT have been banned from use in the United States for decades, other pesticides and most chemical fertilizers have not. Heavy rains wash these agricultural chemicals into our waterways.

Although many chemical fertilizers aren't toxic when applied as directed, they still promote the growth of algae. The algae prevent sunlight from reaching aquatic plants and eventually block the supply of oxygen to aquatic life.

This overenrichment of aquatic habitats, called eutrophication, is a serious threat to many of the Northwest's waterways. One of the most seriously affected was Lake Washington, just east of Seattle.

The population on the eastern shore of Lake Washington had grown from 10,000 in 1940 to more than 120,000 by 1970. Many of the communities around the lake discharged their sewage into the water, which resulted in the disappearance first of the lake's oxygen, then its fish. Water clarity decreased to less than 2 feet, and rampant algae made summer recreational use of the lake nearly impossible.

State legislators eventually passed a bill providing for the construction of four large waste-treatment plants on Puget Sound, and all sewage discharges previously draining into Lake Washington were halted. Within two years, the lake's water clarity had increased to 15 feet, phosphorus levels had dropped from 70 parts per billion (ppb) to 22 ppb, and fish had returned to the lake.

Lake Washington had been pushed to the brink of death and brought back to life again. Unfortunately, not all waterways throughout the Northwest have been so fortunate.

OIL SPILLS

Oil spilled from ships at sea and through mishaps involving offshore oil rigs results in the death of thousands of birds and shore animals each year and may continue to prove deadly to other forms of marine life long after the spill. The worst oil spill in U.S. history took place just 25 miles from Valdez, Alaska.

It started innocently enough at 12:04 a.m. on March 24, 1989, in Prince William Sound off the coast of Alaska. A supertanker, the Exxon *Valdez,* had drifted off course into shallow water. Captain Joseph Hazelwood left the bridge, putting the vessel on automatic pilot and in the hands of a third mate who was unauthorized to navigate in those waters.

Suddenly the *Valdez,* carrying 1,260,000 barrels of oil, ran aground on Bligh Reef, ripping a large hole in its hull and sending oil gushing into the icy waters. Within a week, more than 260,000 barrels of oil (over 11 million gallons!) had been spilled, creating a 50-mile-long slick that sloshed its way to the shores of Katmai National Park, 150 miles from the site of the accident. From there, the oil spread out over nearly 400 miles of Alaska's coastline.

Shortly after announcing the accident, Exxon officials promised the world that they were doing everything in their power to contain the spill and that they fully expected the damage to be minimal. But Exxon, in fact, was making very little headway in controlling the spill. Within a matter of days, the state of Alaska and local fishing boats were forced to take control of the cleanup efforts. By then, most of the damage had been done. The results of nearly 35,000 tons of toxic petroleum released into one of the most environmentally sensitive areas in Alaska were devastating. Salmon hatcheries were ruined. Beaches were covered with tarlike oil that worked its way a foot or more into the sands. At least 23,000 migratory birds, 750 sea otters, and 50 birds of prey had died.

(opposite page)
The oil spill in Alaska's Prince William Sound took a high toll on wildlife.

LONG-TERM CLEANUP EFFORTS

Meanwhile, the same missteps that caused the spill plagued the cleanup and outraged the American public. During the next three months, Exxon spent $115 million (of nearly $2 bil-

lion to date) on additional cleanup efforts. But state and U.S. Coast Guard officials reported that the results of Exxon's efforts had been negligible. Only a few miles of shoreline had been cleaned, and those, ineffectively.

When winter settled over the bay, Exxon and Coast Guard officials were forced to abandon their efforts. The following spring, Exxon announced that it was ready to continue its efforts as various legal proceedings against the oil company made their way through the courts. But by June of 1990, little additional progress had been made, and none is expected. The environment was the big loser in the Exxon *Valdez* disaster.

Despite congressional threats to create laws to prevent future oil-spill disasters such as the one off the Alaska coast, little if anything has been done. Oil-industry spokespersons, trying to calm fears over possible future spills and increased damage to the environment, claim that emergency cleanup procedures immediately following an oil spill can hold damage to a minimum. But environmentalists and the Exxon *Valdez* showed otherwise. The painful truth is that the technology to confine spilled oil to a small, localized area where it can eventually be "mopped up" doesn't exist.

FOOLING WITH MOTHER NATURE

The Pacific Northwest has been a world center for salmon for decades. From Nome, Alaska, to Coos Bay, Oregon, spawning salmon fill rivers, creeks, and streams to bursting. In spots, the fish are so thick that they block the view of the river bottom.

As long ago as 1866, the Northwest's salmon canneries began installing complex mechanized snares at the mouth of the Columbia River and, later, other northwestern rivers to scoop up fish as they moved upstream to spawn. By the turn of the century, the resulting salmon catch topped 1.5 million fish a year. But as the years passed and the numbers of spawning fish decreased, so, too, did the number of salmon caught.

At the same time, several federal agencies were working to make rivers more difficult for fish to live in. The Army Corps of Engineers was assigned to solve the problems of flooding and the blocking of channels by silt from forest destruction and soil erosion. It undertook massive engineering projects to

turn wild, raging rivers into little more than large pools of
dammed water. Together with the Bureau of Reclamation, the Soil Conservation Service, and the Federal Energy Regulatory Commission, the corps built hundreds of dams. These soon destroyed the natural habitat of millions of sturgeon, paddlefish, shovelnose catfish, trout, and spawning salmon, as well as numerous other species of fish. By building dams to eliminate the regular cyclical pattern of flooding along rivers, the federal agencies also destroyed important natural habitat for migrating ducks, geese, and swans that find food, nesting sites, and protection from predators in flooded lowlands.

GOING UNDERGROUND

Throughout the Northwest, as in much of the rest of the world, supplies of fresh groundwater—water stored within the pores of soil and rock formations—are steadily being poisoned by hazardous wastes and chemical pollutants that seep through the soil. Currently, nearly one fifth of the drinking-water wells in Washington and one sixth in Montana contain pollution levels higher than safety limits set by their respective states. Many well contaminants are carcinogenic.

By 1982, chemical pollutants had been detected in the groundwater supplies of 35 states. Although the greatest contributor to polluted groundwater systems are hazardous waste dumps, agricultural chemicals are also major polluters. Yet each year, American farmers spray or spread some 400,000 tons of pesticides and more than 42 million tons of fertilizers on their fields and orchards. Worse, drinking-water protection programs throughout the Northwest leave much to be desired.

In a recent evaluation of the quality of U.S. state programs and policies for drinking-water protection, each state was rated on a scale of 1 to 10, with 10 being perfect. While Massachusetts, Maine, and New Jersey each received ratings of 9 to 10, only the northwestern states of Idaho and Oregon received ratings as high as 5 to 6. Montana, Wyoming, Washington, and Alaska each received ratings of 3 to 4.

Meanwhile, the Northwest continues to poison its underground water supplies. Little is being done even now to monitor the situation and enforce action to stop the pollution.

CHAPTER FIVE

A TIME FOR ACTION

In 1967, the U.S. Fish and Wildlife Service's list of endangered species included 78. Today's list tops 1,200! Endangered northwest species alone include such animals as the short-tailed albatross, American and Arctic peregrine falcons, Aleutian Canada goose, Northern Rocky Mountain wolf, black-footed ferret, Northern kit fox, Columbian white-tailed deer, brown pelican, and grizzly bear. In addition, numerous plants and insects are also on the list.

Although too many people have failed to note this tragic loss of the region's most precious resource, not everyone has ignored the call for action. As long ago as 1860, after President Abraham Lincoln signed a bill creating the first state park in California, Congress designated the land at the headwaters of the Yellowstone River in Montana as America's first public park. The bill created the park for "the preservation, from injury or spoliation, of all timber, mineral deposits, natural curiosities or wonders within said park, and their retention in their natural condition."

(opposite page)
The grizzly bear, already extinct in the lower 48 states, is now on Alaska's endangered species list.

ENVIRONMENTAL ACTIVISTS

Yet environmental action by both state and federal governments has often been slow and ineffective. As an alternative to expensive and time-consuming lobbying and possible legal battles, environmentalists have taken to using other forms of action to create more immediate results.

In the large forested areas of the Pacific Northwest, some environmentalists protesting the widespread use of pesticides have turned to various acts of ecotage—sabotage conducted against environmental polluters in the name of ecology. In 1978, several dozen angry citizens in Keno, Oregon, blocked a public road and fired gunshots into the air in protest of a government spraying campaign. Several others slashed the tires of spray vehicles and set fire to a spray helicopter.

Elsewhere in Oregon that same year, angry citizens petitioned a giant timber corporation whose pesticide-spraying program they claimed caused a large number of pregnant women in a nearby community to miscarry. Protesters were enraged when one of the company's chemists minimized the importance of the issue by stating, "Babies are replaceable."[1]

Another incident—in Index, Washington, in 1980—mobilized 30 women and children who threw themselves on a railway track to halt a 2,000-gallon chemical tanker from spraying the railway right-of-way with chemical herbicides.

Summing up much of the nation's feelings about the chemical spraying of populated areas, Eric Jansson of Friends of the Earth wrote a letter to the EPA that stated, in part, "I would like to suggest that if it is legal to spray people with poison from aircraft and ground rigs without their permission, it should also be quite legal for anyone, including spray victims, to walk into your offices with pesticide cans and spray you with poisons."[2]

But northwestern environmental activists haven't confined their efforts to pesticides. They've also taken aim at one of the most hotly debated issues in the Northwest—nuclear energy.

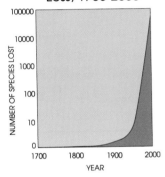

Estimated Annual Rate of Species Loss, 1700-2000

NUMBER OF SPECIES LOST

100000
10000
1000
100
10
0

1700   1800   1900   2000

YEAR

Source: Based on estimates in Norman Myers (ed., *Gaia: An Atlas of Planet Management* (Garden City, NY: Anchor Books, 1984), p. 15

NUCLEAR WASTE HITS HOME

In 1957, a Soviet nuclear reactor plant exploded, releasing highly carcinogenic radioactive fallout into the atmosphere and wiping some 30 towns and villages off the map. Twenty-nine years later, in April 1986, a disastrous nuclear reactor accident at the Soviet Union's Chernobyl plant killed several hundred workers and exposed thousands of residents to radioactive fallout. The ultimate toll from the disaster has been estimated at 135,000 additional cancer cases and as many as 35,000 deaths![3]

The two Soviet incidents were examples of Soviet mismanagement and poor design and construction, according to U.S.

Department of Energy (DOE) officials. Such accidents couldn't possibly happen at nuclear reactor sites in the United States.

Yet several U.S. plants have come dangerously close to major disasters during the last decade. In 1986, residents near the Hanford Nuclear Reservation in eastern Washington had had enough. They began pressuring state and local representatives to close Hanford down. The anti-nuclear activists received support from a 1988 report by scientists working for the DOE, stating that radiation leaks from nuclear-weapons plants such as Hanford might cause abnormally high cancer rates and birth defects.[4]

The Washington plant was one of four nuclear weapons plants targeted for action. Investigators showed that Hanford had been releasing large quantities of carcinogenic radioactive iodine-131 since as far back as 1944. An independent panel investigating one of Hanford's 46-year-old reactors concluded, "The similarities between Chernobyl and Hanford are substantial and make a Chernobyl-type accident at Hanford a distinct possibility, while the differences tend in general to make [Hanford] more, rather than less, dangerous than its Soviet counterpart."[5]

The panel was right. In 1985, a person overseeing the nuclear-weapons facility twice recommended closing the plant's two plutonium factories because of poor design, sloppy and unsafe work practices, and incomplete and false documentation. The report uncovered a weakness in several essential joint welds made by unqualified welders. Further studies revealed that several inspectors had been negligent. In many cases, inspection documents had been dated even before the inspections were actually carried out.

Recent investigations by the U.S. General Accounting Office failed to reveal how much radioactive water has leaked from Hanford and the extent of the seepage into groundwater since nearly half a million gallons of high-level radioactive waste were spilled there in 1956. A 1988 study by the DOE revealed that liquid radioactive and toxic wastes at Hanford had contaminated large underground reservoirs used for drinking water and irrigation.[6]

As a result of these and other findings about the unsafe operating conditions at Hanford, environmental action groups such as the Hanford Education Action League (HEAL), the Natural Resources Defense Council, and the Environmental Policy Institute pressed for Hanford's closing. Following extensive congressional hearings, the federal government finally agreed in 1989 to close four of its largest and most polluting nuclear weapons plants, including Hanford.

THE BIRTH OF A PARK?

Located in southwestern Oregon, the proposed site for a new national park named Siskiyou stretches from the California border to the town of Grants Pass, Oregon. In this vast wild area are the Wild Rogue and Kalmiopsis wilderness areas and the scenic river corridors of the Illinois and Rogue rivers. All these areas are protected from development because of their beauty and ecological importance. By adding the sprawling, mostly undisturbed and still unprotected timberlands that connect the areas, proponents of the new park hope to protect a core of 400,000 roadless acres containing the most diverse mixed conifer forests on Earth.

The region contains every type of outdoor environment imaginable: four wild rivers and cascading white water; huge stretches of old-growth forests with their populations of cougar, bear, osprey, bald eagle, wolverine, and otter; miles of trails winding from rivers to mountaintops; and a sea of native plants and wildflowers—more than 1,400 species identified to date.

As a much-needed economic boost, Oregon's newly proposed park would provide opportunities for scientific research, watershed restoration, recreation, and tourism. By protecting the land from logging and other commercial development, the state would create a solid economy based on sound environmental principles. In return, the park would provide a natural preserve for Oregon's clean air and water, salmon-filled rivers, and numerous species of wildlife.[7]

But the Siskiyou, the largest coastal forest in the continental United States, isn't a park yet. The U.S. Forest Service has long sought the Siskiyou's rich stands of mature timber for logging. At stake are more than 150,000 acres of old-growth trees in nearly all of the region's wildest areas. When the Forest

(opposite page)
The Hanford Nuclear Reservation in Washington state was for years a festering source of radioactive pollutants.

Service began carving a logging road into the forest in May 1983, concerned environmentalists decided to act.

Since it was too late to turn to the courts to stop the construction, Dave Foreman of Earth First! decided on the ultimate weapon—his own body. As a pickup truck filled with workers wound its way down a narrow dirt road, Foreman stepped in front of it. The driver slowed down but kept coming, eventually hitting Foreman in the chest and pushing him back five feet. When Foreman refused to move, the driver accelerated, this time pushing him up a hill until he finally lost his balance. Desperately clinging to the truck's front bumper, Foreman was dragged beneath the engine for over 100 yards. When the truck finally stopped and the workers piled out, the local police placed Foreman under arrest. Foreman's knees suffered permanent damage from the accident, but the road construction was delayed long enough to bring a lawsuit resulting in a temporary injunction against the development.[8]

As the battle between the Forest Service and various environmental groups heats up, the Siskiyou Regional Education Project is soliciting support. (For more information on contacting the association, see the Appendix in this book.) Hanging in the balance is the well-being of the largest center of plant evolution on the West Coast.

SAVING THE SOUND

In 1985, Washington State's Puget Sound Water Quality Authority initiated a program for cleaning up the heavily polluted 3,200-square-mile body of water. The program is funded in part by an 8-cent-a-pack cigarette tax, which generates approximately $8 million a year. The program closely monitors waste from all sources to reduce the flow into the sound.

Besides limiting industrial and toxic waste, the project also includes a program for limiting agricultural runoff. It established strict zoning laws near watershed areas and instituted an area-wide educational program that, in the words of *Time* magazine, teaches everything from the history of the sound to what not to put down the kitchen sink.

Working closely with the project, high school students take water samples and local citizens look for telltale oil spills and

other types of water pollution. According to Thomas
Hubbard, a water-quality planner for the city of Seattle, some of the most effective watchdogs are bridge tenders. "They're up high, and when they see a black scum or a little slick, they let us know about it."[9]

NEW LIFE FOR OLD SALMON

Washington's Elwha River is a centerpiece for the state's million-acre Olympic National Park. Once it provided a passageway to and from the sea for some of the world's largest chinook salmon. But the hundred-pound fish were eliminated from the Elwha when a hydroelectric dam was built to power a pulp mill in nearby Port Angeles.

Environmentalists will be watching closely over the next three years as license renewals come up for the aging Olympic and 200 dams like it scattered across the country. In a surprising move, two federal agencies—the U.S. Fish and Wildlife Service and the National Park Service—are siding with environmental groups in a campaign to tear down the 66-year-old Olympic dam. If they're successful, it will be the first time an existing dam has been torn down for the purpose of environmental restoration.

The U.S. Fish and Wildlife Service is also considering placing several varieties of salmon on the Endangered Species list, giving the federal agency more power in protecting the fish from future hydroelectric and irrigation projects.

"These dams are historical accidents," says Jim Baker of Friends of the Earth, "built during the pioneer days when nobody cared about how much environmental damage they might cause."

Environmentalists believe there's a good chance the dam will be torn down. If they're correct, the mighty chinook will once again be traveling up the Elwha to spawn—for the first time since 1924.[10]

WHAT WE CAN DO

There are many things Americans can do to help save the environment in the Northwest. Here's a list of some of them. For additional information on the subject of environmental issues of concern to the Northwest, as well as on further action, see pages 55-57 in this book.

FOR THE TREES

- Plant and care for trees in your yard and town. A greener America means a more, energy-efficient environment.

- Share your knowledge of trees with your neighbors and suggest that they plant new trees or replace dying ones.

- Join or form a neighborhood or block association whose main goal is the care and planting of trees.

- Involve classmates in tree planting both at school and in the neighborhood.

- Turn down the thermostat at night and whenever the house is empty and close off heat and air conditioning ducts in unoccupied rooms.

- Keep refrigerator cooling coils clean for efficient operation, and set the refrigerator thermostat no lower than 40° F.

- Insulate your hot-water heater and turn its thermostat down to 120°.

- Dry clothes on a clothesline instead of in a dryer.

- Stop using hazardous chemicals in your home. Instead of ammonia-based cleansers, use a mixture of vinegar, salt, and

(opposite page)
Once every year, the U.S. celebrates Earth Day with anti-pollution speeches, plays, and protests.

water for surface cleaning. For the bathroom, use baking soda and water. For an effective wood polish, use a mixture of one part lemon juice to two parts olive or vegetable oil.

- Grow your own organic food whenever possible.
- Eat lower on the food chain—more fruit, vegetables, and grains and less meat, fish, and animal products.
- Shop and play close to home to avoid wasteful automobile trips.
- Bike, walk, carpool, or bus whenever possible.
- Encourage your parents to have their car tuned up every 10,000 miles for maximum performance.
- Tell your parents that radial tires on their car improve gas mileage; encourage them to check their tires' air pressure weekly for maximum efficiency.
- Avoid aerosols and other products containing chlorofluoro-carbons (CFCs), which are damaging to the environment.
- Hold dry-cleaning to a minimum, as the process uses toxic chlorinated solvents.
- Avoid the use of chipboard, plywood, insulation, synthetic carpeting, and upholstery that might contain or create formaldehyde.
- Join at least one environmental organization whose goals and activities you support.
- Hold a contest to see which groups of "junior foresters" can plant the most trees in one school year.
- Ask local businesses and utilities to plant trees on their property and explain why.
- Ask local tree nurseries and garden centers to participate in various tree-planting projects, donating trees or offering them at special discounts.

FOR THE WATER

- Support organizations seeking to ensure the preservation and protection of the Northwest's ocean and coastal resources.

- Write your congressional representative urging increased support for the identification and regulation of pollutants entering coastal areas.

- Save water by finding and fixing leaky faucets.

- Take showers instead of baths.

- Avoid using or disposing of substances that could damage surface water and groundwater.

- Use phosphate-free detergents.

- Dispose of unwanted hazardous household chemicals (such as pesticides, paint remover, and motor oil) at approved community collection points for safe recycling.

- Wash cars and water lawns only when absolutely necessary.

- Landscape your garden to minimize runoff and erosion.

- Avoid using liquid fertilizers, weed killers, and toxic pesticides. Instead, check with your county agricultural department for information about biologically safe alternatives.

- Turn off running water while brushing your teeth or washing dishes to save up to 15 gallons at a time!

- Ask your parents to install water-saving toilets that use 60 to 90 percent less water than conventional models.

IN GENERAL

- Compost your food wastes or put them in the trash instead of in the garbage disposal.

- Avoid using paper or foam cups, towels, and napkins.

- Buy groceries in bulk whenever possible.

- Bring your own reusable cloth shopping bags to the market.

- Buy products that are recyclable, reliable, repairable, refillable, reusable, and in all ways non-disposable.

- Buy beverages in returnable glass containers.

- Buy eggs in paper instead of plastic foam cartons.

- Get a free or low-cost home-energy audit from your local utility company and follow their suggestions.

FOR MORE INFORMATION

The following toll-free hot-line telephone numbers provide information ranging from pesticide use to asbestos in homes; from hazardous-waste disposal to chemical-emergency preparedness.

- Asbestos Hotline (1-800-334-8571). Provides information on asbestos and asbestos abatement programs; Mon. to Fri., 8:15 a.m. to 5 p.m.

- Chemical Emergency Preparedness Program Hotline (1-800-535-0202). For information on community preparedness for chemical accidents, etc.; Mon. to Fri., 8:30 a.m. to 4:30 p.m.

- Inspector General's Whistle Blower Hotline (1-800-424-4000). For confidential reporting of EPA-related waste, fraud, abuse, or mismanagement; Mon. to Fri., 10 a.m. to 3 p.m.

- National Pesticides Telecommunications Network Hotline (1-800-858-7378). Provides information about pesticides, toxicity, management, health and environmental effects, safety practices, and cleanup and disposal; 7 days, 24 hours a day.

- National Response Center Hotline (1-800-424-8802). For reporting oil and hazardous-chemical spills; 7 days, 24 hours a day.

- Superfund Hotline (1-800-424-9346). Provides Superfund information and technical assistance; Mon. to Fri., 8:30 a.m. to 4:30 p.m.

(opposite page)
Scientists spray new plant varieties to determine their resistance to acid rain and other pollutants.

The following list includes organizations that can provide information and materials on various topics of environmental concern in the Northwest.

Alaska Conservation
Foundation
430 W. 7th Ave.
Suite 215
Anchorage, AK 99501
907-276-1917

American Rivers
Conservation Council
801 Pennsylvania Ave.
SE
Washington, D.C. 20003
202-547-6900

Center for Clean Air
Policy
444 N. Capitol St.
Washington, D.C. 20001
202-624-7709

Center for Marine
Conservation
1725 DeSales St. NW
Washington, D.C. 20036
202-429-5609

Citizen's Clearinghouse
for Hazardous Wastes
P.O. Box 926
Arlington, VA 22216
703-276-7070

Citizens for Ocean Law
1601 Connecticut Ave.
NW
Washington, D.C. 20009
202-462-3737

Common Cause
2030 M St. NW
Washington, D.C. 20036
202-833-1200

The Conservation
Foundation
1255 23rd St. NW
Washington, D.C. 20037
202-293-4800

Council for Solid Waste
Solutions
1275 K St. NW
Washington, D.C. 20005
202-371-5319

Defenders of Wildlife
1244 19th St. NW
Washington, D.C. 20036
202-659-9510

Environmental Action
1525 New Hampshire
Ave. NW
Washington, D.C. 20036
202-745-4870

Environmental Coalition
for North America
1325 G St. NW
Washington, D.C. 20005
202-289-5009

Environmental Defense
Fund
275 Park Ave. S.
New York, NY 10010
212-505-2100

Friends of the Earth,
Northwest
4512 University Way NE
Seattle, WA 98105
206-633-1661

Greenpeace USA
1436 U St. NW
Washington, D.C. 20009
202-462-1177

Idaho Conservation
League
P.O. Box 844
Boise, ID 83701
208-345-6933

Izaak Walton League
1701 N. Ft. Myer Dr.
Arlington, VA 22209
703-528-1818

Keep America Beautiful,
Inc.
Mill River Plaza
9 W. Broad St.
Stamford, CT 06902
(Phone # unavailable)

National Association for
Plastic Container
Recovery
5024 Parkway Plaza
Blvd.
Charlotte, NC 28217
704-357-3250

National Audubon
Society
833 Third Ave.
New York, NY 10022
212-832-3200

National Clean Air
Coalition
801 Pennsylvania Ave.
SE
Washington, D.C. 20003
202-543-8200

National Coalition
against the Misuse of
Pesticides
530 7th St. SE
Washington, D.C. 20001
202-543-5450

National Coalition for
Marine Conservation
1 Post Office Square
Boston, MA 02109
617-338-2909

National Geographic
Society
17th and M Streets NW
Washington, D.C. 20036
202-857-7000

National Oceanic and
Atmospheric
Administration
(NOAA)
Rockville, MD 20852
(Phone # unavailable)

National Wildlife
Federation
1412 16th St. NW
Washington, D.C. 20036
202-737-2024

The Nature Conservancy
1815 N. Lynn St.
Arlington, VA 22209
703-841-4860

The Oceanic Society
1536 16th St. NW
Washington, D.C. 20036
202-544-2600

1001 Friends of Oregon
400 Dekum Bldg.
519 Southwest Third
Ave.
Portland, OR 97204
503-223-4396

Puget Sound Alliance
13245 40th St. NE
Seattle, WA 98125
206-343-5865

Sierra Club
530 Bush St.
San Francisco, CA 94108
415-981-8634

Siskiyou Regional
 Education Project
P.O. Box 13070
Portland, OR 97213
503-249-2958

United Nations
 Environment Program
2 U.N. Plaza
New York, NY 10022
212-963-8139

U.S. Dept. of Agriculture
Independence Ave.
 between 12th and 14th
 Streets SW
Washington, D.C. 20250
202-477-8732

U.S. Environmental
 Protection Agency
Region VIII (includes
 MT, WY)
999 18th St., Suite 500
Denver, CO 80202-2405
303-293-1603

U.S. Environmental
 Protection Agency
Region X (AK, ID, OR,
 WA)
1200 Sixth Ave.
Seattle, WA 98101
206-442-5810

U.S. Fish and Wildlife
 Service
Dept. of the Interior
Washington, D.C. 20240
202-343-1100

U.S. Forest Service
P.O. Box 96090
Washington, D.C. 20090
202-447-3957

Washington
 Environmental Council
4516 University Way NE
Seattle, WA 98105
206-547-2738

Wilderness Society
1400 I St. NW
Washington, D.C. 20005
202-842-3400

World Wildlife Fund
1250 24th St. NW
Washington, D.C. 20037
202-293-4800

——— N O T E S ———

INTRODUCTION

1. *The Universal Almanac 1990* (Kansas City, MO: Universal Press Syndicate Company, 1989), p. 314.
2. Ibid, p. 343.
3. Edward C. Wolf, *On the Brink of Extinction: Conserving the Diversity of Life,* Worldwatch Paper 78 (Washington, DC: Worldwatch Institute, June, 1987), p. 7.

CHAPTER ONE: THE WEB OF LIFE

1. *The Universal Almanac 1990* (Kansas City, MO: Universal Press Syndicate Company, 1989), p. 331.

CHAPTER FIVE: A TIME FOR ACTION

1. David Day, *The Environmental Wars* (New York: St. Martin's Press, 1989), p. 219.
2. Ibid, p. 219.
3. *The Washington Post,* May 12, 1988, p. A25.
4. Jon Naar, *Design for a Livable Planet* (New York: Harper & Row, , 1990), p. 159.
5. Ibid, p. 159.
6. Ibid, p. 162.
7. Ibid, p. 119.
8. Ibid, p. 281.
9. Ibid, p. 65.
10. Federal Agencies Target Old Dams To Open up Fish Runs, *"The Denver Post,"* July 15, 1990, p. 14A.

G L O S S A R Y

Acid rain. Rain containing a high concentration of acids from various pollutants such as sulfur dioxide, nitrogen oxide, etc.

Air pollution. The transfer of contaminating substances into the atmosphere, usually as a result of human activities.

Algae. Primitive green plants, many of which are microscopic.

Aquatic. Of or relating to life in the water.

Aquifer. Water-bearing rock or soil.

Atmosphere. A mass of gases surrounding the Earth.

Biome. A specific environment capable of supporting life.

Biosphere. That part of the Earth, including its atmosphere, capable of supporting life.

Carcinogen. A substance known to cause cancer.

Clear-cutting. The practice of cutting all trees and shrubs from the land.

Compost. A fertilizer made up of organic materials.

Core. The center of the planet Earth.

Crust. The outer layer of the planet, consisting mostly of crystalline rocks and including its soil.

Drought. A prolonged period without precipitation.

Ecology. The branch of science concerned with the interrelationship of organisms and their environment.

Ecosystem. A functioning unit of the environment that includes all living organisms and physical features within a given area.

Ecotage. Various acts of protest, legal or otherwise, conducted against environmental polluters.

Energy. The ability to perform work.

Erosion. The removal and transportation of soil by wind, running water, or glaciation.

Eutrophication. A natural process in which lakes gradually become too productive, often due to the introduction of growth-stimulating materials such as phosphates.

Extinction. The disappearance of an organism from Earth.

Fertilizer. A substance used to make soil more productive.

Food chain. A sequence of organisms in which each member feeds on the member below it, such as an owl, rabbit, and grass.

Fossil fuels. Various fuel materials such as coal, oil, and natural gas created from the remains of once-living organisms.

Fungicide. A type of pesticide designed to kill fungi.

Groundwater. Water that is contained in sub-surface rock and soil formations.

Hazardous waste. The extremely dangerous by-product of civilization that, by its chemical makeup, is harmful to life.

Herbicide. A chemical compound used to kill plants.

Homo erectus. Scientific name for one of humankind's ancestral species.

Homo sapiens. Scientific name for modern humans.

Logging. The practice of removing trees, usually selectively, especially for timber.

Magma. Molten rock within the Earth.

Mantle. The part of the Earth situated between the Earth's surface and its core.

Nuclear energy. Energy from the nucleus of an atom.

Nuclear waste. The long-lived, extremely dangerous by-product of nuclear energy or nuclear weapons production.

PAHs. Polyaromatic hydrocarbons. A group of often carcinogenic petroleum derivatives capable of accumulating in organisms.

Particulates. Extremely small bits of dust, soot, soil, etc., that may become airborne.

Pesticide. A general term for any of a large number of chemical compounds used to kill pests such as insects, weeds, fungi, bacteria, etc.

Planetoid. A body resembling a planet.

Pollution. A general term for environmental contaminants.

Power. The rate at which work can be performed.

Recycling. The recovery and reuse of material resources.

Rock. A stonelike material usually composed of a combination of minerals.

Runoff. Water that moves across the surface of the land faster than the soil can absorb it.

Salinization. The increase of salt in soil or water.

Sewage. Refuse liquid or waste matter carried by sewers.

Smog. A visible mixture of solid, liquid, and gaseous air pollutants that are harmful both to human beings and to the environment.

Soil. A living system of weathered rock, organic matter, air, and water in which plants grow.

Strip mining. A method of surface mining that takes in a wide area and is usually used for the removal of coal near the Earth's surface.

Sulfate. A salt of sulfuric acid.

Sulfide. A salt of hydrogen sulfide.

Toxic waste. The extremely dangerous by-product of chemical production or use.

Tundra. A relatively flat, treeless plain similar to arctic or subarctic regions.

Water pollution. The transfer of contaminating substances into water, usually as a result of human activities.

BIBLIOGRAPHY

As We Live and Breathe. Washington, D.C.: National Geographic Society, 1971.

Budiansky, Stephen, and Robert F. Black. "Tons and Tons of Trash and No Place To Put It." *U.S. News and World Report,* Dec. 14, 1987, pp. 58-62.

Day, David. *The Environmental Wars.* New York: St. Martin's Press, 1989.

The Earth Report. Los Angeles: Price Stern Sloan, Inc., 1988.

Grossman, Karl. *The Poison Conspiracy.* Sag Harbor, NY: The Permanent Press, 1983.

Laycock, George. "Trashing the Tongass." *Audubon,* November 1987, p. 110.

Lewis, Thomas A. "Where There's Fire There's Smoke." *National Wildlife,* October/November 1988, p. 16.

Marx, Wesley. "Environmental Countdown." *Reader's Digest,* May 1990, p. 99.

Moran, Joseph M., Michael D. Morgan, and James H. Wiersma. *An Introduction to Environmental Sciences.* Boston: Little, Brown and Company, 1973.

Naar, Jon. *Design for a Livable Planet.* New York: Harper & Row, 1990.

Peterson, Cass. "Scenic Sites under Siege." *National Wildlife,* June/July 1987, p. 44.

Wagner, Richard H. *Environment and Man.* New York: W. W. Norton & Co., Inc., 1974.

Wallace, David Rains. *Life in the Balance.* New York: Harcourt Brace Jovanovich, 1987.

INDEX

Acid rain 31 - 33
Agricultural chemicals 37, 41
Alaska 7, 20, 24, 25, 27, 31, 38, 40, 41
Aleutian Canada goose 43
Algae 8, 11, 19, 37
Antelope 19
Asteroids 7
Automobile exhausts 31, 35

Baker, Jim 49
Bald eagles 24, 46
Beluga whales 36
Bighorn sheep 19
Biome 7
Biosphere 8
Bison 16, 19
Black-footed ferret 43
Black-tailed deer 24
Blackfoot Indians 28
Bladder cancer 36
Blue grouse 24
Brown pelican 43
Bureau of Reclamation 41
Bush, George 29

Carbohydrates 8
Carbon dioxide 8
Carbon monoxide 32
Carbon tetrachloride 28
Carolina parakeets 20
Chemical pollutants 41
Chernobyl 44 - 45
Chestnut-backed chickadees 24
Chevron 28
Clean Air Act 33
Cline, David 24
Coal gasification facilities 35
Columbian white-tailed deer 43
Comets 7
Cougar 19, 46
Coyotes 19
Creosote 36
Crust 11

Dams 41, 49
DDD 37

DDT 37
Department of Energy [DOE] 28, 29, 45
Dinosaurs 8
DNA molecules 36

Eagle Harbor 36
Earth First! 48
Ecotage 43
Elf owls 19
Elk 16
Elwha River 49
Endangered Species Act 49
English sole 36
Environmental Defense Fund 31
Environmental Policy Institute 46
Environmental Protection Agency
  [EPA] 27, 31, 32, 44
Eutrophication 37
Extinction 8, 9, 16, 20, 21
Exxon 38-40
Exxon Valdez 38-40

Federal Energy Regulatory
  Commission 41
Fertilizers 37, 41
Food chain 19, 35 - 36
Foreman, Dave 48
Forest Reserve and Organic
  Administration Acts 20
Friends of the Earth 44, 49
Fungi 8, 33

Gas 7, 8, 28, 35
Glacier National Park 28
Great horned owl 21
Grizzly bears 43
Groundwater 41, 45

Hair, Jay D. 22
Hanford Education Action League
  [HEAL] 46
Hanford Nuclear Reservation 45
Hazardous waste 41
Hazardous waste dumps 41
Hazelwood, Joseph 38
Herrington, John S. 29
Homo erectus 8

Homo sapiens 8
Hydrogen 8

Idaho 7, 20, 22, 28, 41
Idaho Falls 28
Idaho National Engineering
  Laboratory 28
Industrial smokestacks 31

Jansson, Eric 44

Kalmiopsis wilderness area 46
Katmai National Park 38
Kerans, Grattan 33
Kit foxes 19, 43
Koehler, Bar 25

Lake Washington 37
Lincoln, Abraham 43
Lisianski River region 24
Liver tumors 36
Logging 13, 15, 20-24, 46, 48

Malins, Donald 35
Meteoroids 7
Methane 8
Migratory birds 38
Miller, George 27
Missoula [MT] 32
Montana 7, 20, 28, 31, 32, 36, 41, 43
Moose 16
Mountain lion 19

National Audubon Society 24
National Park Service 49
National Wildlife Federation 22
Natural Resources Defense
  Council 46
Nitrogen 8
Northern Rocky Mountain wolf 43
Nuclear power 28
Nuclear weapons' plants 28

Offshore oil rigs 38
Oil 27, 28, 35, 38, 40, 49
Oil spills 27, 38, 49
Old-growth forests 20 - 24, 27, 46
Olympic National Park 49
Oregon 7, 12, 15, 16, 20, 25, 33, 36, 40,
  41, 44, 46
Osprey 46
Owls 16, 19
Oxygen 8, 36, 37

Pacific Northwest Research
  Foundation 35
Paddlefish 41
Particulates 32, 33
Passenger pigeons 20

Paul, Liz 29
Peregrin falcon 43
Pesticides 37, 41, 43, 44
Plutonium 28
Polyaromatic hydrocarbons
  [PAHs] 35-36
Polycyclic organic matter 32
Prince William Sound 38
Prudhoe Bay 27
Puget Sound 36-37, 48
Puget Sound Water Quality
  Authority 48

Radioactive waste 28, 45
Red-breasted sapsuckers 24
Rocky Mountains 31
Roosevelt, Theodore 20

Salmon 19, 24, 38, 40, 41, 46, 49
Sea otters 38
Seattle 31, 35-37, 49
Sewage 35, 37
Short-tailed albatross 43
Siskiyou 46-48
Snake River Alliance 29
Snake River Aquifer 28
Soil Conservation Service 41
Soil erosion 15, 16, 41
Southeastern Alaska Conservation
  Council 25
Special Isotope Separation [SIS] 28
Spotted owl 16, 21-22
St. Lawrence River 36
Strip-mining 36-37
Sulfates 36
Sulfides 32-33, 36
Sulfuric acid 36

Timber wolves 16
Tongass National Forest 24-25
Toxins 36

U.S. Coast Guard 40
U.S. Department of the Interior 27, 36
U.S. Forest Service 20-27, 28, 46, 48
U.S. General Accounting Office 45

Vancouver Canada geese 24

Washington 7, 12, 16, 20, 36, 37, 41, 44,
  45, 48, 49
Weaver, Jim 25
Wild Rogue 46
Willamette Valley 33
Wolverine 46
Wyoming 7, 20, 31, 36, 41

Yellowstone River 43